Disney's Year Book 1999

Published by Grolier Books

Grolier Books is a division of Grolier Enterprises, Inc.

FERN L. MAMBERG	*Executive Editor*
S. J. VICTORIA VERNER	*U.K. Editor*
ELIZABETH A. DEBELLA	*Designer*
BARBARA L. PERSAN	*Production Manager*

ISBN: 0-7172-8847-1
ISSN: 0273-1274

Stories on pages 16–27, 38–49, 60–71, 80–91, and all Disney character illustrations copyright © 1999 by Disney Enterprises, Inc.

Pages 16-27 written by Catherine McCafferty; Pages 38-49 written by Amy Bauman; Pages 60-71 written by Victoria Saxon; Pages 80-91 written by Liane Onish. All stories illustrated by The Alvin White Studio.

Illustration Credits and Acknowledgments

6—The Granger Collection; 7—© Stock Montage; Courtesy, The Oakland Museum of California; 8—© Stock Montage; 9—Arnold Fisher/Science Photo Library/Photo Researchers, Inc.; M. Claye/Jacana/Photo Researchers, Inc.; 10—© Stock Montage; 11—© Barbara Stitzer/ PhotoEdit; 12—© J. H. Carmichael, Jr./Bruce Coleman Inc.; 13—Del Mulkey/Photo Researchers, Inc.; © David T. Roberts/Photo Researchers, Inc.; 14—© Jane Burton/Bruce Coleman Inc.; 14–15—© Joe McDonald/Bruce Coleman Inc.; 15—© Ron Garrison/Zoological Society of San Diego; 28–29—From *Make Sculptures!* © 1991 by F&W Publications. Used by permission of North Light Books, a division of F&W Publications, Inc.; 30—© Earth Satellite Corporation/ Science Photo Library/ Photo Researchers, Inc.; 31—© Mark Spencer/AUSCAPE; © Gregory Ochocki/ Photo Researchers, Inc.; 32—©Superstock, Inc.; © Superstock, Inc.; © Jon Levy/ Gamma Liaison; 33—Artist, Vince Caputo; 34—© Nancy Simmerman/Tony Stone Images; 35—© Tom Bean/DRK Photo; © Tom & Pat Leeson/Photo Researchers, Inc.; © Gregory Ochocki/Photo Researchers, Inc.; 36—© John Cancalosi/Peter Arnold, Inc.; © J. C. Carton/Bruce Coleman Inc.; 37—© Stephen Frink/Waterhouse Stock Photography; © R. Andrew Odum/Peter Arnold, Inc.; 50—Reuters Archive Photos; 51—© Brock Peter/ Gamma-Liaison; 52—© Ravell Call/Gamma-Liaison; 53—© Archive Photos; 54—© Carlos A. Angel/ Gamma Liaison; 55—Smithsonian Institution; The Granger Collection; 56—Everett Collection; © AP/Wide World Photo; 57—© Kennan Ward/ Bruce Coleman Inc.; 58—© Bruce Roberts/Photo Researchers, Inc.; 59—© Michael Fogden/Bruce Coleman Inc.; © Fritz Polking/Peter Arnold, Inc.; 72-73—Designed and created by Jenny Tesar; 74-75—© Tim Davis/Davis/Lynn Images; 75—© Stan Osolinski/ Oxford Scientific Films; 76—© Tim Davis/Photo Researchers, Inc.; 77—© David Fritts/ Tony Stone Images; © Leonard Lee Rue III/Animals Animals; 78—© C. Greg Gilman/ FPG International; © Norbert Rosing; 79—© Ron Gordon Garrison/ Zoological Society of San Diego; 92—© Agence France Presse/Corbis-Bettmann; © Al Bello/Allsport; 93—© Allsport; 94—© Agence France Presse/Corbis-Bettmann; Shaun Botteril/ Allsport; © Jamie Squire/Allsport; 95—© Shaun Botteril/ Allsport

Contents

THE CALIFORNIA GOLD RUSH

"Gold!" It was a magic word. In 1848, the discovery of this glittering yellow metal in California started America's first gold rush—and opened the Far West to settlement almost overnight. It was one of the most important events in U.S. history. In 1998, people celebrated the 150th anniversary of that discovery. And they looked back to the time when gold fever swept the nation.

It all started on January 24, 1848, at Coloma, a small town not far from Sacramento. A carpenter named James Marshall was at work building a sawmill on the banks of the American River. The mill belonged to John Sutter.

Marshall was inspecting the mill's water channel when he

News of the discovery of gold in 1848 at Sutter's Mill (right) spread quickly. By the following year, tens of thousands of "forty-niners" were trying their luck in California's gold fields (left). Almost overnight, the quiet village of San Francisco became a busy boomtown (below).

Gold seekers came from far and wide. They loaded up their gear on pack burros and headed into the hills. Prospecting, they soon found, was hard work.

suddenly spotted something glittering in the stream. He stooped for a closer look. Could it be gold? It was—and within just a few months the rush was on! By the end of the year, there were thousands of California miners at the gold fields.

Back east, few people believed the stories about the gold. But in December, President James K. Polk mentioned California's "abundance of gold" in a speech. People thought that if the president believed the stories, they must be true. Gold was just lying around on the ground. All you had to do was pick it up!

Gold fever swept America and the world. Workers left their jobs. Soldiers deserted their posts. People sold everything they owned to get money for the trip west. Nothing mattered except gold.

But first they had to get there.

There were only three ways to get to California from the East Coast. And all were dangerous. Some prospectors sailed around the stormy tip of South America, a five-month voyage. Others went by steamship to Panama and then crossed the isthmus by mule. (The Panama Canal hadn't been built yet.) Then they waited for a steamship to take them to San Francisco. Still others headed right across the continent by wagon. This was the fastest route, but prospectors faced scorching deserts, towering mountains, and attacks by outlaws.

A Fool for Gold

A miner dips a flat pan in a mountain stream. He swirls and tilts it to rinse away the silt. And there, in the bottom of the pan, is the gleam of yellow he's been looking for. It's gold! Or is it?

Newcomers to the gold fields were often misled by "fool's gold," or iron pyrite. Iron pyrite is yellow and shiny, just like gold. But real gold is soft, and fool's gold is brittle and crumbly. If you hit it gently with a hammer, it breaks. And iron pyrite isn't worth anything.

The picture below shows a chunk of gold. Above is iron pyrite. Would *you* be fooled by fool's gold?

But none of that stopped the gold seekers. In 1849, 80,000 people—called "forty-niners"—poured into California to look for the wealth in the ground. And they came from as far away as Britain, Canada, South America, Australia, even China.

When the forty-niners reached California, they found that the gold wasn't just lying around. Most of it was in mountain streams, mixed in with sand and gravel. The prospectors had to pan for it—they used an ordinary flat pan to wash the soil away from the gold particles. Or they used other, larger devices that did the same thing. And once the surface gold was found, they had to dig with picks. It was backbreaking work.

Many prospectors used a device known as a cradle. They rocked the cradle—which was filled with gold, water, and gravel—until the gravel washed out, leaving the heavier gold.

Few prospectors actually struck it rich. Still, fortunes were made. In 1852, the peak year, the gold fields produced £20 million. One mine yielded a single nugget worth more than £10,000. But soon, big mining companies took over. Only they had the money and equipment to operate deep mines.

And that was the end of the gold rush.

But the gold rush changed California for ever. Thanks to the huge numbers of gold seekers, it was admitted to the Union as a state on September 9, 1850. Today, more than 30 million people live there. And it all started when Americans and other people all over the world dreamed of gold—and believed that with a pan and a little luck, anyone could strike it rich!

Yellow Gold and Blue Jeans!

Are you wearing a bit of history? It could be—if you're wearing blue jeans. Blue jeans

go back to California gold rush days. Among those who went to California then was a German-born businessman named Levi Strauss. He sold work clothes and other supplies to the miners.

In 1872, a tailor told Strauss how to make work pants that were extra strong: Put copper rivets at the corners of pockets and other stress points. And Strauss used blue denim because it was a tough material. Soon blue jeans became favourites with miners, cowboys, workers, and people everywhere. And they've never gone out of style!

This kinkajou uses its tongue to lap up a tasty meal of insects. But animal tongues are meant for more than just getting food and eating.

Your tongue helps you taste, chew, and swallow food. A tongue also helps animals eat. And some animals, like the kinkajou shown above and the lorikeet shown on page 15, use their tongues to *get* food, too. But animals can do other, even more amazing things with their terrific tongues.

The giraffe, for example, uses its 20-inch black tongue like a flyswatter to flick insects away from its nose. It can even use its tongue to remove bugs from inside its nostrils. And the gecko uses its tongue as a windshield wiper. This lizard has transparent eyelids that don't move. They stay over the eyes to protect them. When the eyelids become dirty, the gecko licks them clean with the tip of its tongue.

The hedgehog uses its tongue to avoid

The giraffe (above) and the gecko (left) use their tongues to clean themselves.

13

A hedgehog (above) uses its tongue to lick saliva onto its spines to hide its scent. A snake (right) uses its tongue to pick up the scent of prey. And a lorikeet (opposite page) uses its brushlike tongue to gather pollen.

enemies. The prickly little animal chews or licks flowers, earthworms, rotten meat, and even soap. This creates a lot of saliva. The hedgehog then uses its tongue to toss the foamy saliva over its spines. The smell of the saliva hides the hedgehog's real scent from enemies.

The snake uses its forked tongue to pick up the scent of prey. It flicks its tongue back and forth, gathering tiny chemical particles of scent from the air. Then it draws its tongue into its mouth and places the tips into two small holes in the roof of the mouth. These holes work much the way your nose does. When the snake smells a mouse or other prey, it prepares to strike.

You can't clean yourself with your tongue. And you can't track an animal with it. But your tongue does something that no

animal tongue can do. It allows you to speak. Without your tongue, you wouldn't be able to form many words. So you see, you, too, have a terrific tongue!

WORTHY WARRIORS

Yao, Ling, and Chien-Po tried. They really tried to live up to their new duties as the Emperor's personal guards. But their responsibilities in the palace were very different from their old duties on the battlefield. Here, they had no Huns to defeat. They had only the Emperor to guard. And while Yao, Ling, and Chien-Po knew that was very important, they also knew that it was not as exciting as their days with Mulan.

"I wish Mulan were here," Chien-Po sighed as he and Yao stood guard outside the Imperial dining room. They watched Ling and the Imperial chef bring the Emperor's lunch.

Yao sniffed the air. "Rice! Remember that first day we met Mulan? When we got into trouble over the rice?" He laughed. "What a fight that was! Ha! Yah!" Yao kicked the air as Ling and the chef drew closer.

"Yao. . ." Chien-Po warned.

But he was too late. Yao's foot kicked the rice bowl out of the chef's hands. It landed at the feet of Shang, their captain, who was coming to see the Emperor.

"Yao," said Shang, "Have you forgotten how to be an Imperial soldier?"

"No," said Chien-Po. "The rice reminded us of Mulan."

"And the fight we had," Yao added.

Shang folded his arms. "Did it also remind you that you had to pick up every single grain of rice that day?"

When no one answered, he said, "Very well, then. If you need rice to remind you of Imperial discipline and duties, you should not be guarding the Emperor. You can guard his pantry. And you can start now."

But Yao, Ling, and Chien-Po did no better guarding the Imperial pantry. The rice only reminded them of how hungry they were. The tea reminded them of how thirsty they were. At the end of their first week on pantry duty, the royal chef complained to Shang, "They are eating us right out of the palace! At this rate, we won't even have enough food for

the Emperor's birthday banquet!"

Shang found the three pantry guards snoring at their post, with three empty bowls in front of them. "Enough!" Shang shouted, jolting them awake. "I am giving you one final chance to prove yourselves worthy of Imperial duty. The Emperor would like Mulan to share his birthday celebration. I want the three of you to bring her back here. If you can't do that, do not bother to return!"

Yao, Ling, and Chien-Po rode away from the palace quietly. "Will Mulan be willing to return to the Imperial City?" Ling asked finally.

"When she went home. . ."

The three of them stopped. ". . .she said her place was with her family, not with the Emperor's Council," Chien-Po finished.

Ling thought for a moment. "Well, Mulan doesn't have to know that the Emperor wants to see her. We could just say that we need her help."

Yao snorted. "That's the truth. Between you drinking the Emperor's tea, and Chien-Po eating the Emperor's rice—"

"And you spilling the Emperor's rice," said Ling.

"We are all to blame," said Chien-Po. But Yao and Ling were already fighting. They tangled and tumbled all the way to Mulan's door.

"Yao! Ling! Chien-Po!" Mulan welcomed them into her family's home. "How is life in the Imperial City?"

"It's. . .very full," said Ling, thinking of all the rice. "But we need your help to deliver a special birthday gift to the Emperor."

"What gift is that?" asked Mulan.

Ling thought quickly. "Fireworks! We are going to make the best fireworks display ever. And we thought that since you used fireworks so well against Shan-Yu—"

"That you would help us," Yao said.

They held their breath as they waited for Mulan's answer.

"I suppose I could help you with the fireworks," Mulan said finally. "But then I must come straight back. You know that my place is here."

"But—" Yao began.

"But we need to get fireworks now," said Ling. "We'll leave for the Imperial City as soon as we get them."

The three sighed with relief as they left Mulan's house. "We'll work out the rest later," Ling promised.

Night was falling when Mulan and her friends reached the Imperial City. The streets were crowded with people eager to

celebrate the Emperor's birthday. Yao, Ling, and Chien-Po pushed through the throng and approached their captain.

"It is a good thing that you have proved yourselves worthy as Imperial soldiers," Shang told them. Then he frowned at the

wagon load of fireworks. "But why did you bring fireworks? We already have a royal display arranged. And where is Mulan?"

Yao, Ling, and Chien-Po turned to find Mulan. But she was gone! "She was right here. . ." Ling stammered. "We must have lost her in the crowd!"

"I warn you," Shang told them. "If this is a trick. . ."

Yao and Chien-Po lit torches and searched the shadows. "This is all your fault," Yao told Ling.

"My fault?" said Ling. "You went along with it! Now we'll never be Imperial soldiers again!" Yao leaped at Ling. As Chien-Po reached to stop him, he dropped his torch on the fireworks cart.

Whizzz! BANG! Poppp! Hsss! Brilliant fireworks blazed above the palace.

"What are you doing?" Shang asked. "It isn't time for the fireworks yet!" he said. "And again—where is Mulan?"

Yao, Ling, and Chien-Po smiled weakly.

"We. . ." said Yao.

"She—" said Ling.

"Silence!" Shang ordered. "I asked you to bring Mulan at the

Emperor's command! By failing to do so, you have disgraced yourselves! From now on, you will work in the Emperor's rice fields!"

Suddenly Mulan hurried up. "I'm sorry! I know I promised to help you with the fireworks," she gasped. "The crowd was so thick I couldn't reach you in time. But your display was very beautiful.

"Oh, hello, Shang," she said shyly.

The fireworks faded. In the sudden silence, the Emperor spoke. "What a magnificent display! It reminds me of Mulan's

defeat of the Huns. Her bravery saved our Empire. I wish she could be here tonight. I am older now, and I may not see such a hero again in my lifetime."

Then Mulan understood. She stepped up in front of the Emperor's throne. She bowed deeply. "I am honoured that you would share your day with me." Then she stood and smiled at Yao, Ling, and Chien-Po. "But there are others I must honour, too. Yao, Ling, and Chien-Po brought me here today. They

fought with me to save the Imperial City." Mulan turned to Shang. "And Captain Shang led us to victory."

The Emperor smiled. "I am honoured many times over to have such fine Imperial Guards in my palace."

Yao, Ling, and Chien-Po nudged one another. "We're back in the palace!" Ling said.

Yao nodded. "I knew it would work out."

"It was my idea about the fireworks," Ling said.

"Your idea?" Yao scoffed. "Your idea almost got us—"

Chien-Po wrapped his strong arms around their shoulders. "Brothers," he said, "It is *my* idea not to ruin our last chance to be Imperial guards."

And to Shang's surprise, they never did.

LET'S STUFF IT!

Stuff big paper cut-outs with paper scraps and turn them into the pictures shown on these pages—a spaceship, a cat, a fish, and even your best friend!

WHAT YOU NEED TO MAKE "SOCCER BOY":

Large sheets of paper	Stapler
Paper scraps for stuffing	Scissors
	Glue
Paints	Stick
Paintbrushes	Decorations, such as
Felt-tip pens	wool and a bandage

1. Place two big sheets of paper on the floor. Ask a friend to lie down, and trace around him.

2. Colour the tracing. Add lots of details to make it look like a real person.

3. Staple together the two sheets of paper in a few places. Cut the "person" out of both sheets at once.

SPACESHIP TO THE MOON

FAT CAT

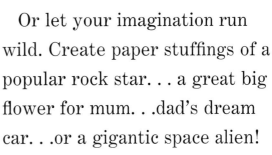

Don't feed the Fat Cat and Smiling Fish. They're already stuffed!

SMILING FISH

Or let your imagination run wild. Create paper stuffings of a popular rock star. . . a great big flower for mum. . .dad's dream car. . .or a gigantic space alien!

4. Put lots of staples around the edges of the head. Stuff. Then staple and stuff another small area.

5. Use a stick to push paper scraps into hard-to-reach places. Finish by stapling the last opening.

6. Glue on some decorations—wool on the hair, fringed paper eyelashes, and a bandage.

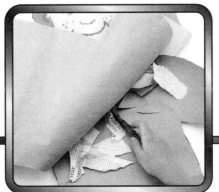

From space, Earth looks like a big blue ball because of the ocean waters.

Year of the Ocean

The Water Planet! That's what aliens on some distant planet might call Earth if they could see it through a telescope. No wonder. Nearly 70 percent of Earth's surface is covered by the oceans—the Atlantic, Pacific, Indian, Arctic, and Antarctic Oceans. To draw people's attention to the importance of these salty seas, the United Nations declared 1998 the International Year of the Ocean.

Why is the ocean so important to the world's people?

🐚 Without the ocean, life couldn't exist on Earth.

🐚 The ocean is a major source of food. And as the world's population grows, so does the demand for fish.

🐚 Lots of other products come from the ocean, too. For example, a substance that comes from red algae is used to add smoothness to toothpaste and peanut butter. Other substances are used in medicines. And the ocean contains useful minerals such as sand and gravel and sulphur and tin.

Delicate Coral Reefs

Coral reefs are found in warm ocean waters throughout the world. The plants and animals that live there make the reefs look like beautiful underwater gardens.

Coral reefs are formed by tiny creatures called coral polyps. Each polyp has its calcium skeleton on the outside of its body. When the polyp dies, its skeleton remains. And as more and more skeletons pile up, the reef grows. Over centuries, a coral reef can stretch for miles.

In recent years, these delicate habitats have been dying out. Scientists think that pollution or the sun's ultraviolet rays are responsible.

The ocean affects us in many ways. It gives us fish for food. It's a great place for fun sports like scuba diving. And ocean temperatures and currents affect the weather, contributing to storms like tornadoes.

○ The ocean is home to such appealing sea mammals as whales, dolphins, seals, and sea lions. Dolphins, with their lively ways and intelligence, seem especially to fascinate us.

○ The ocean is a major force behind the weather. Rain and snow begin as water vapour that has evaporated from the ocean surface. And changes in the ocean's temperature and currents help cause droughts, floods, hurricanes, and tornadoes.

The ocean is an important transportation route. New cars, clothing, television sets—all sorts of products—are carried worldwide by ships.

In coastal areas, the ocean is a place for fun. Swimming, sailing, fishing, scuba diving, and other water sports draw people to the sea.

While people enjoy and benefit from the ocean and its marine life, they have sometimes harmed them, too. For example, many of the fish that we eat are caught in giant nets that can pull in up to 300,000 pounds of fish at a time. As a result, many species of fish that were once plentiful are now rare.

Pollution is also harming the ocean. Oil spills from

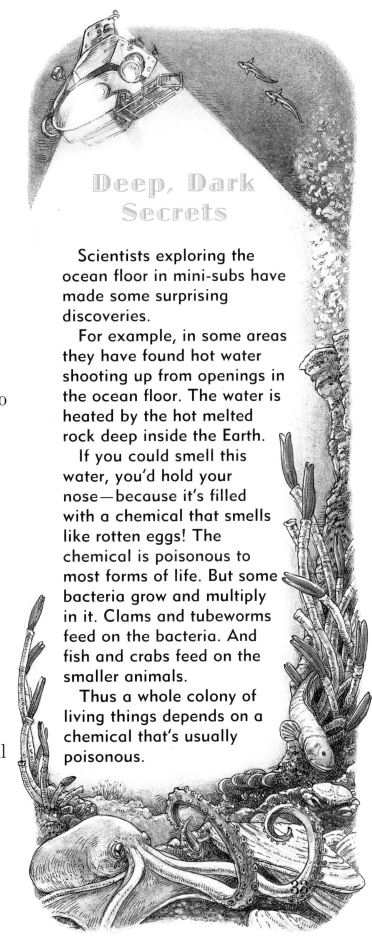

Deep, Dark Secrets

Scientists exploring the ocean floor in mini-subs have made some surprising discoveries.

For example, in some areas they have found hot water shooting up from openings in the ocean floor. The water is heated by the hot melted rock deep inside the Earth.

If you could smell this water, you'd hold your nose—because it's filled with a chemical that smells like rotten eggs! The chemical is poisonous to most forms of life. But some bacteria grow and multiply in it. Clams and tubeworms feed on the bacteria. And fish and crabs feed on the smaller animals.

Thus a whole colony of living things depends on a chemical that's usually poisonous.

ships are killing marine life. So are pesticides and fertilisers that are washed into the sea by rain. In addition, torn nylon fishing nets and other junk that people have left or tossed into the sea can trap or choke marine animals.

Global warming is a worldwide warming trend resulting from air pollution. It is already causing some polar glaciers to melt. As glaciers melt into the ocean, the sea level rises. The sea also becomes less salty. This could cause changes in ocean currents and affect the weather.

The focus of the International Year of the Ocean was to find ways to control overfishing, pollution, and threats to marine life.

Today, fish are caught by the ton—which threatens marine life.

Marine Life in Trouble

Getting rid of junk in the ocean has become a major problem. And polluting the ocean doesn't just cause scenes of great ugliness. It also hurts marine life. For example, if junk such as a nylon fishing net is left in the ocean and washes up to shore, seals and other animals can get tangled up in the net and be harmed.

You can help. Never leave rubbish behind, in the water or on the beach.

Its message was this: The ocean is essential for life on Earth. We must learn about it. And we must understand how our activities affect it. Then we'll be better able to protect it.

When Spanish explorers first came to the Americas, they saw a mammal covered with bony plates. They named it the **armadillo**, or "little armoured one." Most armadillos have a solid shield over the shoulders. Another shield covers the rear part of the body.

The **snail** has a hard coiled shell on its back. The shell is attached to the rest of the body by a muscle. When danger threatens, the snail pulls itself into the shell. As the snail grows, its body produces material that makes the shell grow larger, too.

Animal Armour

It isn't easy for animals in the wild to stay alive. There are enemies everywhere. But all creatures have ways to defend themselves. One of the best defenses is a tough covering—a kind of animal "armour." Porcupine quills and turtle shells are well-known examples. But there are many other kinds.

As it swims through a coral reef, the **parrot fish** is protected by hard overlapping scales. The scales cover the parrot fish from head to tail, acting like a suit of armour. And because the scales are flexible, they allow the fish quickly to dart away from a bigger fish looking for a meal.

The **spiny lizard** loves to crawl onto a rock or tree stump and lazily soak up some sun. Hungry animals may see it there. But they keep their distance because the spiny lizard is well named—its body is protected by large scales that end in sharp points.

Spiders, insects, shrimps, and some other animals are protected by hard skeletons that cover the outside of the body. These are called exoskeletons. Snails and clams also wear their skeletons—called shells—on the outside. And many fish are protected by armourlike scales on their skin. Sometimes these scales are pointed or tipped with spines. For all these animals, their "suits of armour" help them to stay alive another day.

Tink Gets Her Jingle Back

Not long after Wendy, John, and Michael Darling returned from Never Land, Peter Pan appeared at their nursery window again one evening. Everyone was asleep, but Wendy—ever watchful for Peter—heard his whispered call.

"We need your help, Wendy," Peter said. Only then did Wendy see Tinker Bell's bright glow; she hadn't heard the pixie's familiar bell-like voice.

"Tink's lost her voice," Peter explained, "and she insisted you were the only one who could help her."

"Of course I'll help," Wendy answered, waking her brothers. She turned to Tinker Bell in time to see her give a great, big sneeze. "Oh, dear! Tinker Bell must have caught a cold! Hmmm."

Tink crossed her arms over her chest and glared at Wendy, blinking rapidly.

"Tink says only humans 'lose' their voices because of colds," Peter translated. "She says her voice is *really* lost. We have to find it and reattach it—just the way you did with my shadow."

"Find her voice? Reattach it?" Wendy exclaimed. "Goodness! I think she'd be better off drinking hot tea and getting some sleep. But if she thinks searching will help, that's what we'll do. Where shall we start?"

Tinker Bell zoomed across the room again, blinking more rapidly than before. This time she was excited.

"Slow down, Tink!" Peter sighed. Even without her jingling bell, he was able to understand his winged friend, but it was hard when she blinked so fast.

"She says her voice is out there somewhere," Peter said, pointing to the darkened city of London.

Wendy sighed. "It's a big city," she said. "Let's get started."

With a happy twirl, Tinker Bell sprinkled pixie dust over everyone, and they rose into the air alongside Peter. One by one, they flew out of the window to soar high above the city streets.

"Did you hear that?" Wendy shouted suddenly when they'd flown some distance from the Darling home. She circled in the air, and everyone pulled up beside her to listen. Sure enough, a delicate jingling sound arose from the park below.

"That sounds about right," Peter said, cocking his head to one side to hear the sound better.

Tinker Bell nodded and excitedly led the group down, where they found. . .a cat!

"That's certainly not Tinker Bell's voice," Michael exclaimed. "It's the bell from that cat's collar."

The tabby glanced up at the group and then dashed into the bushes. They could hear the frantic "jingle, jingle" of its collar long after the cat was out of sight.

"Well, that was just our first try," Wendy said cheerfully. "Let's keep looking."

With a whoosh, everyone rolled skyward. They were soon even farther from the children's quiet little street and their warm beds. It was then that they heard a second bell tinkling.

"Down there!" Peter called. He zipped down through the clouds. John, Wendy, and Michael—and Tinker Bell—were on his heels when they discovered that this "voice" was a. . . carriage bell!

"Git up, there," the carriage driver called to his horse. He made a clucking noise and tugged on the reins. The bell jingled as the old horse clip-clopped off.

"That's not Tink's voice, either," Peter said, sitting down on a cloud. As Wendy, John, and Michael gathered around him, Tinker Bell fluttered slowly up to the group, looking tired. She sneezed three times—silently, of course—and rubbed her eyes.

"Oh, Peter," Wendy whispered. "I'm certain Tinker Bell has a cold and that's how she lost her voice. Can't you make her rest?"

Peter laughed. "You can't make Tink do anything she doesn't want to do," he said.

"Then we'll have to go on looking to keep her spirits up until her voice returns," Wendy decided. She jumped into the air. "Come on, everyone! We've got a long way to go tonight."

Tinker Bell was the first to lift into the air. She gave Wendy a shy smile and then zoomed ahead, her bright light leading the way. The group wound its way across the night sky behind her, flying up one street, down another, across this meadow, and back over that forest. Even as morning approached, they kept on following each bell they heard, sure that it would be the right one.

One bell, they discovered, belonged to a cow named Doris. It hung from a rope tied at her neck and clanked as the old girl moved about. Up close, it didn't even sound right.

Another bell turned out to be the bell over a bakery door. It jangled each time someone went in or out—although, at this hour, when most people were still sleeping, it wasn't ringing a lot.

44

"The wind must have made it ring," said Michael.

They found a church bell, a bicycle bell, a bell attached to a garden gate, and even an old ship's bell that rang as the boat rocked gently in the river. But none was Tinker Bell's voice.

The pixie's wings drooped as they discovered yet another bell that wasn't hers. By now the rising sun was sending its rays over the horizon. Soon she and Peter would have to leave.

"Don't give up hope, Tinker Bell," Wendy said. She held out her hand and, to her surprise, the pixie landed on her finger-tips. "You can come back tonight, and we'll search again."

"Yes," John added. "We'll keep looking until we find your voice, no matter how long it takes."

"Of course we will," Wendy said as they turned for home. "Wait! There's one more bell to check. But it's kind of far away. Tinker Bell, why don't you curl up in my pocket where it's quiet and warm until we get there?"

To everyone's surprise, Tink did as Wendy suggested. Once inside the pocket, the fairy was asleep almost immediately.

"Well, look at that!" Peter whispered. He turned to Wendy. "We'd better hurry, Wendy. Tink and I don't have much time left."

Wendy led them back. They flew across the meadow, over the river, back into the heart of London, and right up onto the face of the biggest clock in the city. The big clock hands ticked to the hour just as they arrived. Its huge bell began ringing.

Just then, Tinker Bell awoke from her nap. With a yawn, she climbed to the edge of Wendy's pocket and launched into the air. Her light blinked madly as she flew round the clock.

"What's she saying?" Wendy shouted over the clock's noise.

Peter chuckled with Tinker Bell, who was looping through the air, rolling with laughter. "She's wondering how you could have thought this huge bell could be her voice."

The clock hit its last note, then fell silent.

"That's funny," John said, "The clock stopped, but my ears are still ringing."

"Mine, too!" Michael laughed.

Wendy shook her head. "That ringing isn't your ears! It's Tinker Bell! She has her voice back!"

It was true. Tinker Bell's high, sweet voice rang out clearly. Still jingling, she landed on Wendy's shoulder.

"Tink wants to know if you really thought this bell was hers," Peter told Wendy.

Wendy smiled at Tinker Bell. "No. I knew this bell was much too big to be your voice. I also knew that, with a little time and sleep, your voice would be fine. I'm sorry to have tricked you."

Tinker Bell smiled, jingling, and kissed Wendy's cheek. Then she yawned.

"Tink doesn't mind, Wendy," Peter answered, yawning, too.

"We really must get home, Peter," Wendy said, "and you and Tinker Bell must hurry back to Never Land."

With that, Peter and Tink, Wendy and John and Michael rose one final time into the air and headed home to their warm beds and sweet dreams.

British driver Andy Green hits 763 miles an hour in the *Thrust Super-Sonic Car.* It was the first car to go faster than the speed of sound.

GOING SUPERSONIC ON WHEELS

For Andy Green, October 15, 1997, was a day to remember. As a British Royal Air Force fighter pilot, he had often flown faster than the speed of sound. But on this day, he *drove* faster than the speed of sound. He became the first person to go supersonic on wheels!

How fast is the speed of sound? That depends on how high above the Earth you are and what the temperature is. High in the sky, the air is thin and cold. There, a pilot has to fly at about 660 miles per hour (mph) to go faster than the speed of sound. That's slower than on land, where the air is thicker and warmer.

Andy Green raced his car in the Black Rock Desert of Nevada. The speed of sound there was about 748 mph. He went faster than that, though. On two 13-mile runs, he averaged 763 mph!

And when he set the record—Boom! Boom! People nearby heard loud, thunderlike noises called sonic booms. When a vehicle moves at supersonic speeds, it creates waves of air called shock waves. It's these shock waves that cause sonic booms.

Cars have certainly come a long way since they were first invented a hundred years ago. At that time, people pottered around at a few miles an hour. But some daredevils soon began setting speed records. The 100-mph mark was reached in 1904, 200 mph in 1927, and 300 mph in 1935.

The *Thrust SSC* is like a jet aeroplane without wings. That suited British fighter pilot Green down to the ground.

Other milestones weren't set for nearly 30 years, when U.S. driver Craig Breedlove began to race a new kind of car. Called the *Spirit of America,* it had jet engines, just like an aeroplane. Breedlove quickly broke the 400-mph mark in 1963, 500 mph in 1964, and 600 mph in 1965.

British driver Richard Noble also raced a car with jet engines. He called his the *Thrust SuperSonic Car.* In 1983, he set a new land speed record of 633.5 mph and was dubbed the Fastest Man on Earth. Soon, Noble and Breedlove set their sights on the next records: 700 mph—and the speed of sound. But it took many years for the two men to accomplish this.

Craig Breedlove was the first man to go faster than 400, 500, and 600 miles per hour. But Andy Green beat him to the sound-barrier record.

In 1997, the British and American speedsters brought their cars to Black Rock Desert—about the smoothest, flattest place in the world. It's great for high-speed racing.

A year earlier, Breedlove had wrecked the *Spirit of America* while doing 677 mph. Though he had completely rebuilt the car, mechanical problems meant that his fastest run in 1997 was 636 mph.

Meanwhile, Richard Noble had decided not to race himself. He chose Andy Green, an RAF pilot, to drive the *Thrust SCC*. Green unofficially broke the sound barrier on October 13. Because the team took 50 seconds too long to turn the car around, the record didn't count. But two days later, Green rocketed through the sound barrier and into the history books—at an astonishing 763 mph.

Chuck Yeager—
Supersonic Flyer

On October 14, 1947, a B-29 bomber carried a small rocket plane called the X-1 to an altitude of 26,000 feet. Inside the X-1 was U.S. fighter pilot Chuck Yeager. When the X-1 was dropped from the B-29's bomb bay, Yeager fired the rockets and the X-1 shot ahead. He became the first person to fly faster than the speed of sound. One historian called the flight "the most significant event in the history of aerospace. . . between the Wright brothers and the landing on the moon."

On October 14, 1997, the day before Andy Green broke the sound barrier on land, Yeager climbed skyward in an F-15 jet fighter. To celebrate the 50th anniversary of his historic flight, he broke the sound barrier once again—at the age of 74!

It's a Record!

Jesus David Reyes Díaz of Bogota, Colombia, set a new world record in 1997. At the age of 3 years, 9 months, he was recognized as the world's youngest billiard player. That didn't surprise young Jesus. He had been playing billiards since he was 1½! And like so many other record-breakers, his action made its way into the famous *Guinness Book of World Records*.

Jesus's record was excellent. But records of all kinds are being set, and broken, practically every day. People are fascinated by these champions—we love to know whatever or whoever is biggest, smallest, fastest, slowest, oldest, youngest, or best!

The Hope diamond is the most popular museum object in the world. Every year, about 6 million people see this glittering gem at the National Museum of Natural History in Washington, D.C. It holds another record, too: At 45 carats, it's the world's largest blue diamond.

Queen Victoria ruled Great Britain from 1837 until her death in 1901. She was queen for 63 years, 7 months, and 2 days. That made her the longest-reigning British monarch—and the longest-reigning queen of any land. She came to the throne when she was 18 years old, and died at the age of 81.

In 1998, the movie *Titanic* sailed into the record books. First, people spent more money on tickets for *Titanic* than on any other movie ever made. And its 11 Academy Awards tied the record set by the 1959 movie *Ben Hur*. *Titanic's* Oscars included Best Picture, Best Director, and Best Original Song.

Why did *Titanic* set so many records? Because the film seemed to have something for everyone. The story was about a real event—the sinking of the ship *Titanic* by an iceberg in 1912. And it had eye-popping special effects and heart-stopping suspense. Perhaps most of all, the movie was also a tender love story, featuring Leonardo DiCaprio and British actress Kate Winslet.

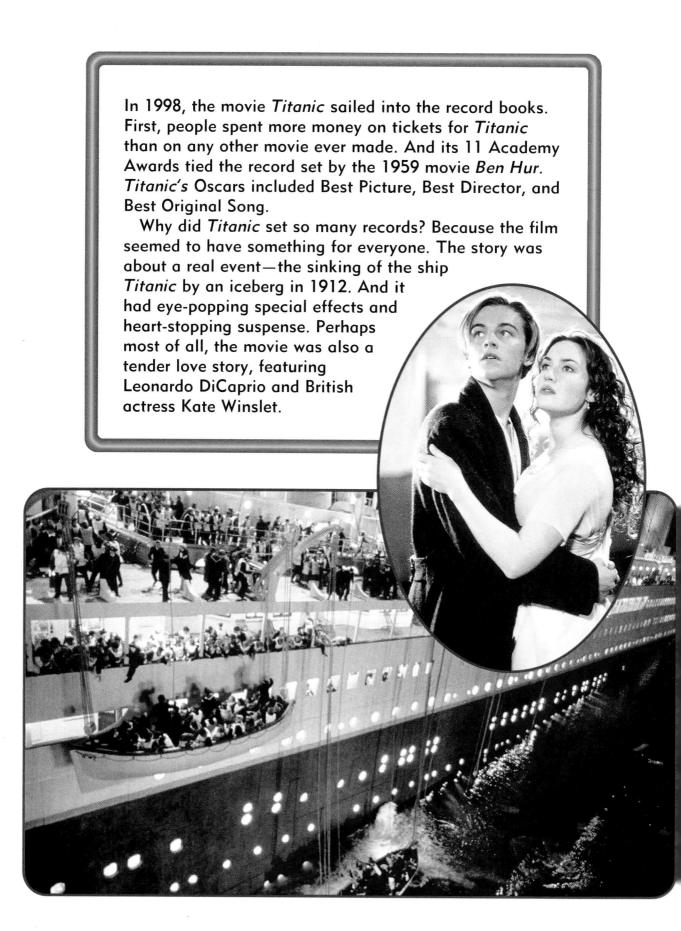

Bristlecone pines hold the record as the longest-living trees. Some are almost 5,000 years old. This makes them the oldest living things on Earth!

Bristlecones grow on high mountain slopes in the western United States—where they live through icy winters, sizzling summers, strong winds, and frequent droughts. They grow very slowly. In 100 years, their trunks may become only an inch thicker. The twisted shapes and many bare branches of these amazing trees show how hard they fight to stay alive. But bristlecone pines are tough. They can survive even if all but a few of their branches and roots die.

Elvis Presley burst onto the rock music scene in 1956. By the time of his death in 1977, he had recorded more than 170 hit singles and 80 top-selling albums. More than a billion copies of his records have been sold. That makes him the most successful solo recording artist ever!

Elvis was the top teen idol of the 1950s. Some of his most popular songs were "All Shook Up," "Hound Dog," and "Heartbreak Hotel." He also made a number of movies. Elvis Presley's records still sell today, and to his fans he remains the "King of Rock 'n' Roll."

The three-toed sloth holds a strange place in the record books. It's the slowest mammal in the world! The shaggy creature lives in the rain forests of South America. It spends most of its life hanging from tree branches—inching along at about 15 feet a minute. And it sleeps about 20 hours a day. The animal's slow-moving, sleep-loving habits gave rise to its name—the word *sloth* means "laziness."

The elegant cheetah is the world's fastest land mammal. On the African plains where they live, cheetahs have been clocked at speeds of up to 70 miles an hour. That's more than twice the speed of the fastest human sprinter—and about 400 times the speed of a three-toed sloth.

A LITTLE HELP FROM A FRIEND

"Yippee!" Kiara exclaimed. "C'mon, Daddy, wake up! You promised we could walk the Pride Lands together. Today's a perfect day!"

Kiara's father, Simba, stretched and gave a great big yawn. Kiara shuddered. Her father's yawn always sounded like a roar to her. Someday she, too, would have a big roar like her father's. Then all the animals in the Pride Lands would respect her. She would be able to go wherever she wanted whenever she wanted.

When Kiara and Simba stepped outside, Timon and Pumbaa were waiting for them.

Kiara sighed. She knew why they were there. When would everybody stop treating her like a baby?

Just then Zazu flew up to Simba. "Sire!" Zazu exclaimed. "Some Outsiders have been spotted in the Pride Lands—near the western canyon. You'd better come at once."

Simba turned to Kiara. "I'm sorry," he said. "Our walk will have to wait."

"That's okay," Kiara answered. "I'll just hang out around here. I won't go too far. I promise."

But Simba knew his daughter's adventurous spirit all too well. "Just stay in sight of Pride Rock at all times. And take Timon and Pumbaa with you wherever you go."

"Aw, Daddy," Kiara complained.

"Kiara, I don't have time to discuss this," Simba said. "Just do what Timon and Pumbaa ask you to do."

Kiara watched her father head off on another adventure. Why couldn't she go with him? She could help him chase all those mean Outsiders right back to their home in the Outlands.

Then Kiara had an idea. She thought she could remember how to get to the western canyon by herself. All she would have to do was lose Timon and Pumbaa somewhere along the way. That should be easy enough. She'd certainly done it plenty of times before.

"Wait for us!" Timon and Pumbaa shouted as they scrambled after her. Soon the trio was crossing a wide, grassy plain.

"Hey, Timon," Pumbaa said as he looked at a grove of trees. "Isn't that where we found all those juicy grubs last week?"

"Pumbaa, Pumbaa, Pumbaa," Timon said. "Which one of us knows where to find grubs?"

"Well, you do, Timon, but—"

"So let me tell you about those trees over there, Pumbaa," Timon said. "Those trees—hey! That's where we found all those grubs last week. Pumbaa, I'm a genius!"

Timon hopped onto Pumbaa's back. "To the grubs, Pumbaa!"

Then Timon turned to Kiara. "Follow us, Princess. You're about to experience a feast fit for the future queen!"

Kiara followed them—but only because she knew this would be her best chance to escape.

Sure enough, as soon as Timon and Pumbaa found their grubs, they completely forgot about Kiara. The lion cub quickly slipped away through the trees, giggling to herself.

Suddenly Kiara heard a growl. Then a ball of fur tackled her, rolling her over and over. When Kiara caught her breath, she was looking into the eyes of a male lion cub not much bigger than she was. He was trying to look very ferocious, but he had mud on his nose. And his growl sounded feeble. Kiara couldn't help it. She had to giggle.

"What are you laughing at, Pride Lander?" the other cub snarled.

"Well. . ." Kiara hesitated. "Actually, I was laughing at you." Then she burst out in another round of uncontrollable giggles.

The other cub sneered grumpily. Then he looked more closely at Kiara. He had met her once before. She was the one who had taught him to play tag!

"Kiara?" the cub asked. "Hey! It's me—Kovu!"

"Kovu?" Kiara said. "Cool! I was wondering if I'd ever see you again!"

"Hey, want to play tag? I loved playing that game, and none of my friends knows how to play, so—"

"Oh, my gosh!" Kiara interrupted. "I can't play. I was on my way to find my dad. He went to chase some Outsiders away from the western canyon. Want to come along?"

"Nah," said Kovu. "I'll just stay here by myself."

"Why?" asked Kiara. "It'll be totally cool. They'll go, 'Roar!' and then my dad'll go, 'ROARRRRRR!' Then those Outsiders are going to turn into a bunch of scaredy cats, and my dad'll chase them all away!"

"Kiara, I'm an Outsider. Remember?"

"Yeah, but—but you're not like the other Outsiders, Kovu. You're fun," Kiara replied.

"Aw, forget it," Kovu said. "Go on. I don't need to play with you anyway. I have plenty of things to do here by myself."

Kiara started to leave. Then she stopped. It really would be more fun to stay and play with Kovu.

Kiara raced back to Kovu and tapped him on the back. "You're it!" she cried as she raced away.

Kovu gave chase. "I'll get you!" he cried. Suddenly both cubs came to a halt.

"What was that noise?" asked Kovu.

"It sounds like. . ." Kiara hesitated. Then she knew what the sound was. It was Pumbaa! And he was in trouble.

Kiara and Kovu ran toward the sound of Pumbaa's voice. They found him pacing around at the base of a tree, looking up helplessly.

"Pumbaa, what's wrong?" Kiara asked.

Pumbaa explained. Timon had climbed the tree to find some good bugs, but had lost his balance. He'd hit his head on a branch and knocked himself out. Luckily his foot had become tangled in a vine. Timon hadn't fallen, but now his foot was slipping out of the vine loop.

Kiara knew she had to help. This would take some fast thinking. Hmmm. . .

Suddenly she had an idea!

Kiara turned to Kovu and asked him to climb the tree. Then she jumped on top of Pumbaa's back. Now she was just inches away from Timon. When Kovu had climbed high enough, Kiara asked him to chew right through the vine holding Timon's foot. When Timon fell, he landed safely on Kiara's back, but he still wasn't very alert.

"C'mon, Kovu," Kiara urged as she headed back to Pride Rock with her two baby sitters. "We need to get help for Timon."

"I don't think I'd better come with you," Kovu replied. "I don't think an Outsider would be welcome in the Pride Lands."

Kiara looked back at her friend. "I guess you're right." She sighed. "See you later, then."

"Hey, Kiara!" Kovu called to her. "You were really great. That was some quick thinking you did."

"Thanks." Kiara smiled. "You did some quick climbing."

On the way back to Pride Rock, Timon began to feel better. Pumbaa told him all about how Kiara had saved him.

"Gee, Kiara," Timon said. "Maybe next time you should be *our* baby sitter."

Kiara beamed with pride.

"But let's agree not to tell Simba about the Outsider, okay?" Timon added.

When the trio reached Pride Rock, Simba was waiting for them. The warning about the Outsiders had been a false alarm.

When he heard what had happened, Simba turned to his daughter. "You must have thought quickly to save Timon," he said. "I'm very proud of you."

Kiara looked at Pumbaa and smiled. Then she thought of Kovu. "It was nothing, Dad. It just shows what you can do with a little help from your friends."

TAKE NOTE!

You can use your favourite stickers to create all kinds of cool things—including these eye-catching sticker notecards!

To make a notecard, take a sheet of coloured paper and fold it in half. Then fold it in half again.

Decorate the front of the card with fun stickers, showing balloon-carrying bears or happy frogs or chugging trains—anything that appeals to you. Or make designs using little sticker hearts, dots, and stars. Use felt tip markers to add extra details.

Finally, open the card and write a note to a special friend or family member.

A word from the wise old owl . . .

WANNA PLAY?

Wolf cubs chase each other outside their den, pretending to bite without hurting each other. A cheetah cub pounces on a stick and bats it around. A young antelope bounds into the air, runs, and leaps up in the air again. And baby hippos challenge each other in a game that looks like head wrestling.

What are all these animals doing? They're all playing—and having a wonderful time at it!

74

Many animals, especially young mammals, love to play. But their play is more than fun. Play trains them to become grown-ups. It helps their brains to develop. And it helps them learn the skills they will need to survive in the wild.

Play, for example, helps animals learn how to hunt for food. That's why lion cubs play rough games.

Primates—humans, monkeys, and apes such as the orangutans shown at left—are among the most playful animals in the world. But many other kinds of animals, like the lion cubs shown below, like to play, too. And their rough-and-tumble play teaches them skills that will help them survive as adults.

They stalk, chase, and pounce on each other. And they bat and "catch" sticks, stones, feathers, and leaves—even their own tails. They're using the skills they'll need when they become adults and are ready to stalk and capture prey. Land mammals like lions aren't the only animals that do this. Dolphins, for instance, also play hunting games. When they leap out of the water and play underwater tag, they are sharpening their fishing skills.

Other animals eat plants, not meat, so they don't need to learn how to catch prey. But they need to know how to avoid being the prey of some other animal. For example, as young mountain goats playfully leap from ledge to ledge, they're learning how to get away from the cougars, wolves, and bears that might want to eat them. Young horses, antelopes, and

Dolphins sharpen their fishing skills as they frolic in the water and play underwater tag.

A mountain goat playfully leaps from ledge to ledge. This helps it develop the balance it needs to stay alive in its rugged mountain home.

sheep experiment with other ways of getting away from predators. They race around, chasing each other, leaping, and kicking out. Their high-speed games help them develop quick reflexes and strong running muscles.

WHERE'S MY TOY?

Animals not only play with each other—they also play with toys. This young wolf uses a stick to start a chase game. It may "dare" another wolf to take the stick, but then run away with it. Whales have been seen playing with balls of kelp. And elephants have been spotted hurling clods of earth with their trunks.

A playful baby rhino runs rings around its mother and butts her until she lets out a grunt that means "Stop that!"

Animal play has still other purposes. It teaches animals how to defeat a rival. It helps them learn how to court a mate. And, for animals that live in groups, play helps them form bonds and get along with others. This is important because

Bears and dogs are known enemies. But sometimes odd playmates come together. In Canada's far north, this bear lumbered over to a place where about 40 sled dogs were tied up. The bear and the dogs romped and played together for more than a week.

young animals that play together—wolf cubs, for example—will one day hunt together in a pack.

Adult animals are usually too busy finding food to spend much time playing. But sometimes they get into the act, too. Like adult humans, many adult animals seem to love playing with their babies. Mother brown bears enjoy rolling around with their cubs and giving them gentle bear hugs. Some gorillas play peek-a-boo with their offspring. Even the tough rhinoceros enjoys some horn-to-horn fun and games with its young.

For animals young and old, fooling around is lots of fun—but the games are usually a matter of survival!

PLAY "TALK"

Animals have special ways of telling each other that they feel like having fun. Here's how some of them say, "Let's play!"

- A panda does a somersault to let others know that it wants to romp.
- Horses leap, buck, or shake their heads.
- A kitten taps another kitten with its paw.
- A weasel arches its back and hops.
- A dog or wolf does a play bow, crouching down in front with its tail waving in the air.
- Mountain goats rear up on their hind legs or lean to one side.

Maid Minnie and the Earl of Edam

Prince Pete was busy prying into his father the King's private papers. Suddenly he came upon a letter from Maid Minnie's parents. It had been written eighteen years ago, shortly before they died. "Ah-ha!" he cried when he had finished reading the letter. "I see that I must marry Minnie!" The Prince was greedy, not for love but for wealth and power. He had never given the orphaned Maid Minnie a second thought—until now.

"The King and Queen request that his highness Prince Pete and their beloved ward, Maid Minnie, attend a royal family meeting in the royal family room!" announced the royal crier.

"What? Another royal family meeting?" Pete grumbled.

Maid Minnie had just returned from her morning ride. She dismounted and headed for the royal family room.

"How was your ride, my dear?" asked the Queen.

"Did you happen to meet Mickey, Earl of Edam, again?" guessed the King with a wink.

Maid Minnie blushed just as Prince Pete stomped in.

"The Queen and I have been invited to Bath to visit Lady Bubble and Sir Toyboat," the King announced. "And you, my son, will rule until we return."

Prince Pete smiled—a particularly nasty smile, Maid Minnie thought.

Outside the castle another meeting of sorts was taking place. "Come on, already!" squawked Friar Duck. Mickey sighed and followed his friend back to Edam.

"Why can't you fall in love with a princess? Someone with money?" Friar Duck complained. "Your castle turrets are leaking, your drawbridge is warped, and. . ."

But Mickey wasn't listening. He was daydreaming about his one true love, Maid Minnie.

Early the next morning, after the King and Queen had left for Bath, Maid Minnie saddled up for her daily ride. Much to her surprise, Prince Pete was in the stable.

"What a fine day! I shall ride with you," he said grandly.

"How. . .kind," she replied suspiciously.

When they were out of sight of the castle, the Prince smiled as sweetly as he could (which was not very) and said, "Maid Minnie, when shall we get married?"

Maid Minnie said, "When we find our one true love."

Prince Pete laughed. "You misunderstand me, my lady. By 'we,' I mean yourself, Maid Minnie—and me."

"But I don't love you," said Maid Minnie.

"Deep in my, er. . .heart, I have always loved you, dearest Minnie, although I may not have shown it," Pete assured her.

"I am sorry, Your Highness," Minnie said, "but my answer must be no."

Prince Pete was prepared for her refusal. He had another plan. "So be it," he said. "Oh, I almost forgot—this letter came for you today."

"It's been opened!" she accused. The Prince just smiled.

"Dear Maid Minnie," Minnie read. "You must come to Bath. The Queen needs you. Signed, Lady Bubble."

"How odd," thought Maid Minnie.

Prince Pete was quite pleased with his forgery. Neither of them knew Lady Bubble or her handwriting.

"I'm sure she means for you to leave immediately," said the Prince, pretending concern. Just then, a carriage and two of Prince Pete's soldiers appeared. "Go now. I shall send your things later."

Maid Minnie felt something was definitely not right.

The Prince led Minnie's horse back to the castle, smiling to himself. His soldiers would take her to his hunting lodge and keep her there.

As the Prince entered the castle, he pretended alarm.

"Maid Minnie has been maid-napped!" he cried. "The bandits demand gold for her release! Send word throughout the kingdom: Triple taxes must be paid in gold, and at once!"

The castle was a flurry of activity. Messengers raced off with letters to all the lords in the kingdom. Prince Pete appeared upset, but inwardly he was extremely pleased with himself.

The carriage carrying Maid Minnie rushed past Sir Mickey without stopping. Thinking quickly, Minnie tossed her handkerchief out the window.

Sir Mickey picked it up. "Maid Minnie is in that carriage," he said. "Where is she going?" He turned his horse and galloped back to his own castle. Then he, Friar Duck, and a dozen soldiers set out after the carriage.

The fastest carriage is no match for soldiers on horseback. When the soldiers stopped the carriage, Maid Minnie quickly jumped out. "Oh, Sir Mickey!" she cried. "Something is not right. Prince Pete gave me a letter from Lady Bubble saying the Queen needs me in Bath. Why didn't the Queen write to me herself?"

Sir Mickey frowned. "The Queen did not write because she is not in Bath," he revealed. "The royal carriage broke down near Edam. The King and Queen are staying with *me* until their carriage is repaired."

Sir Mickey and Maid Minnie reached Edam castle just as the message from Prince Pete arrived. Friar Duck read it aloud: "Maid Minnie has been maid-napped! To pay her ransom, all taxes are hereby tripled and must be paid at once." The letter was signed King Pete.

"*King* Pete? Maid-napped? Ransom?" cried the King.

Maid Minnie said, "What can we do?"

"We'll storm the castle!" squawked Friar Duck.

"The Prince has many soldiers," the King pointed out.

"I have a plan," said Sir Mickey.

The next day, seventeen cloaked figures entered the throne
room, carrying chests that held not gold but rocks painted gold.
"For Maid Minnie's ransom, Prince Pete," said one muffled
voice. So eager was Prince Pete for the gold that he stepped
down from the throne. As he did, two cloaked figures circled
behind him and sat on the thrones. The other figures
surrounded the greedy prince.

"Now!" a voice cried. Quickly, they all tossed off their cloaks,
revealing Sir Mickey, Friar Duck, the King and Queen, Maid
Minnie, and twelve of Sir Mickey's soldiers!

Standing before the King and Queen, Sir Mickey held Prince
Pete at sword-point.

"Prince Pete, we strip you of your title," proclaimed the angry king. "Henceforth you shall be Plain Pete, formerly known as Prince."

As Plain Pete was led away, the King said, "Name your reward, Sir Mickey."

Friar Duck whispered, "The turrets are leaking, the drawbridge is warped. . ."

"I want no reward, Sire," Sir Mickey said.

"Would you accept gold and land as the dowry of your bride-to-be?" suggested the King.

Sir Mickey blushed. "No, Sire. For Maid Minnie is the one and only true love of my life."

The Queen smiled and said. "The dowry is Minnie's."

"What?" exclaimed Minnie and Mickey together.

The Queen explained. "When Minnie's parents died, they left her wealth and kingdom to us until she was of age. To keep her from fortune hunters, we kept her royalty a secret, even from her. We hoped she would find a husband who would lovingly care for her and her people. I believe Princess Minnie has found such a man."

From that day on, Minnie, formerly known as the Maid, became Princess Minnie.

A week of wonderful wedding celebrations followed. Even Friar Duck was happy. And the leaking turrets and warped drawbridge of Edam castle were finally repaired.

The 1998 Winter Olympics

The 18th Winter Olympic Games were held in Japan, in February 1998. The official site was the city of Nagano on Honshu, Japan's main island. Surrounded by the beautiful snow-covered Japanese Alps, Nagano was the perfect setting for the opening ceremonies,

Top: Dancing round the world.
Bottom: Lighting the flame.

which celebrated peace and friendship throughout the world. In one of the most colourful events, dancers joined hands around a huge balloon representing Earth. Then, Japanese figure-skater Midori Ito—who had won the silver medal at the 1992 Winter Games—lit the Olympic flame. And the exciting competitions and breathtaking performances began.

The Olympic Mascots

Sukki, Nokki, Lekki, and Tsukki were the official mascots of the snowy 1998 Winter Olympics. These colourful, cuddly characters looked like baby owls, or owlets. So they were called "Snowlets." Images of the Snowlets appeared on toys, pins, dolls, and many other items. But the most popular souvenirs of the Winter Games were stuffed Snowlets.

About 2,450 athletes from 72 nations took part in 68 events. Germany won the most medals—29, including 12 golds. Two very popular events were figure skating (because of its grace and beauty) and bobsledding (because of the breakneck speed of the sport). Two of these performances are described here.

Icewoman. All eyes were on U.S. figure-skater Tara Lipinski. She leaped and twirled as gracefully as a dancer. And she landed seven perfect triple jumps—including the triple-loop, triple-loop combination she's so well known for. As a result, six of the nine judges gave her first-place votes. At

British 4-Man
Bobsled Team

age 15, Tara became the youngest person ever to win the gold medal in Olympic figure skating.

Icemen. Bobsledding is one of the fastest and most thrilling winter sports. Bobsled teams race down ice-covered chutes at 80 mph. In the 4-man event, the British team of Sean Olsson, Dean Ward, Courtney Rumbolt, and Paul Attwood had a terrific first-round race—only 7/100 of a second behind Germany, the eventual gold-medal winner. After two more dramatic rounds, Britain shared the bronze medal with France.

Olympic Snowboarding

Snowboarding was the most popular new sport at the 1998 Winter Olympics. Snowboarders

ride a single wide ski that's like a surfboard or skateboard.

There were two exciting Olympic competitions. One event (the giant slalom) involved zigzagging around poles while racing downhill at high speeds. In the other event (the freestyle half-pipe), snowboarders did acrobatic flips and twirls while racing downhill. Shown here is Ross Rebagliati of Canada, who zigzagged his way to the gold in the men's giant slalom.

THE JOKE'S ON YOU!

What did the teddy bear say when he was offered dessert?

No, thanks, I'm stuffed!

What did the duck say to the shopkeeper?

Put it on my bill!

What did the reeeeally big spider spin?

The World Wide Web!

What member of a cricket team wears the largest hat?

The one with the largest head!

What happens to a frog who's parked illegally?

It gets toad away!

What can fall down and never get hurt?

Snow can fall down and never get hurt!